AFFIRMATION FOR BUSINESSMAN

I am a Super Successful Businessman.

Money flows to me easily and effectively.

All my business needs are met on time.

My business is profitable to consumers.

I gain a lot personally and monetarily.

My clients are always happy with me.

My customers are family to me.

I am a perfectionist in execution.

My Marketing skills are awesome.

My sales are always achieved well before the last date.

My Operations team works very hard.

My Research and Development is through.

My Human Resource Management is perfect.

My Accounts and MIS are accurate.

My Leadership and Management is the best.

I have gained mastery over my mental, physical,

emotional and spiritual aspects.

I plan my future well in advance.

I daily do Introspection before sleep.

I plan my day after I wake up.

I am regular in my affirmations.

I repeat my affirmations 3 times a day.

I love my team.

I respect my team.

I love and respect my clients.

I maintain work life balance.

I live my life around my business.

The whole world is my client.

People trust me.

I am the greatest businessman ever lived.

So be it.

Thank you. Thank you. Thank you.

Done. Done. Done.

<u>Affirmations for Filmmakers</u>

I am a great Filmmaker.

My films are entertaining.

People love to watch my films again and again.

People are always waiting for my films.

People of all ages watch my films.

My films are great films.

I utilize the opportunity of being a filmmaker.

My films guide people in their lives.

My actors truly portray what I aspire.

Great stories come to my mind.

My direction team is excellent.

We make films for all platforms and theatres.

My films are dubbed & sub-titled in all languages.

My script is top notch.

Songs of my film become legends.

I am a legendary filmmaker.

I get millions of dollars for filmmaking.

My producers have faith in me.

My financers always make money.

Film Industry has become a family.

I receive awards and rewards for my work.

I am nationally & internationally acknowledged.

I maintain a good work life balance.

I complete a film a year.

I receive active as well as passive income.

I am the controller while doing a project.

All things fall for me at the correct time.

I am a famous person.

I am a Money Magnet.

So be it.

Thank you. Thank you. Thank you.

Done. Done. Done.

<u>Affirmations for Best Selling Author</u>

I am a Best Selling Author.

Millions of copies of my book have been sold.

Readers download the Kindle edition.

Readers give my books to friends & colleagues.

Sales of the book are permanent in nature.

Readers read my previous books.

My books are sold every day.

People discuss about me and my books.

I receive prizes, awards and rewards every day.

My fan club has crossed 1billion readers.

My books are translated in almost all languages.

My books change the lives of people who read them.

I bless all those who buy my books.

My book captures the reader's mind.

My writing is natural and in constant flow.

My proofreaders are very good.

My publishers are making great money.

My publishers are honest & pass on the royalty on time.

I love to go to Book Inaugurations Celebrations.

My book gets good reviews.

My fans buy my books in Pre Sale.

My fans email me regarding the book.

Almost all books are converted into films.

Hollywood & world cinema are attracted to my books.

Pre-offer for making a film in my book always comes.

Publishers offer me money for writing books.

My publishers organize public talks for me.

My books are on the front page

of Amazon, Flipkart, and Websites.

Every library has my books collection.

I maintain work life balance.

My family loves what I do.

I am a Money Magnet.

I am the greatest author ever born.

So be it.

Thank you. Thank you. Thank you.

Done. Done. Done.

<u>Affirmations for Great Actor</u>

I am a great actor.

I love my profession.

I am born to be a star.

I will leave a legacy after me.

My films will inspire others.

I am a Legend.

My work is admired all over the world.

People are immediately attracted to me.

My fans are growing rapidly.

People run towards me when they find me.

People take selfies with me.

I am popular in all classes.

Producers have faith in me.

I am the first choice of all the directors.

I am working in Hollywood/Bollywood.

My income increases day by day.

I am always paid up front.

I finish my projects in time.

My films always recover their cost.

Universe gives me what is best for me.

Great scripts come to me.

Writers write stories for me.

I am the most popular actor.

People book advance tickets for my films.

I contribute a lot to society.

I do a lot of charity work.

I maintain work life balance.

I do regular exercise.

I am a Money Magnet.

So be it.

Thank you. Thank you. Thank you.

Done. Done. Done.

Affirmations for 8 Pack Body

I love my body.

I go to the gym.

I exercise my body.

On Monday I do my legs.

On Tuesday I exercise my chest.

On Wednesday I exercise my shoulders.

On Thursday I exercise my back.

On Friday I do triceps and biceps.

On Saturday I go for cardio.

On Sunday I relax my body and

take a massage or sauna bath.

I complete my warm ups before exercise.

I do stretching after exercise.

I take my whey protein after the exercise.

I have my vitamins, calcium & antioxidants on time.

I drink 12-15 glasses of water daily.

I have a great body.

My body is well proportioned.

My 8 packs look beautiful.

My chest is attractive.

My t-shirts look good on me

because of my triceps and biceps.

My sex life is great.

I have great stamina.

My body adds to my personality.

I look handsome and charming.

People are attracted to me.

Girls are charmed by my physic.

Every cell of my body vibrates with joy.

My heart pumps my blood to each

and every corner of my body.

All organs are in harmony.

I look young and younger.

So be it.

Thank you. Thank you. Thank you.

Done. Done. Done.

<u>Affirmations for Receiving Love</u>

I am lovable.

I am ready to receive love.

I am kind and loving.

I am talented.

I am Intelligent.

I am Creative.

I am attractive.

I deserve the very best in life.

I have a great deal to share with others.

I have a lot to offer.

Everyone recognizes my efforts.

Everyone loves me.

I love the world and the world loves me.

I am willing to be happy.

I am willing to be successful.

I am creating more positive & loving self-image.

I am a good friend.

Friends share their things with me.

I keep their secrets with me.

People accept me as I am.

I am a brilliant and interesting person.

I like myself very much.

I am so warm and loving.

People appreciate good things in me.

People love my sensitivity.

People love my honesty.

I do not please anyone.

I express myself freely, fully and easily.

I am a powerful being.

I am ready to receive love.

I am a love magnet.

So be it.

Thank you. Thank you. Thank you.

Done. Done. Done.

<u>Affirmations for Teachers</u>

I am a good teacher.

I give my best to my students.

I believe in a student's future.

I research new ideas for students.

I prepare well before taking my classes.

I teach my students how to lead a good life.

I am a positive teacher.

I am an optimistic teacher.

I look at all students unbiased.

My life is dedicated to students.

I give value to my students.

I refer positive books to my students.

I encourage students to become independent.

I discover latent talents of my students.

I ask students to do what they love.

I give good practices to students.

Students are directed in the right path.

I teach students to become Entrepreneurs.

I ask my students to travel all around.

I teach my students to earn a lot of wealth.

I teach my students that money is power.

I encourage students to get the power to do whatever they want in life.

I am a positive mind teacher.

I have a responsibility for great teaching.

My students will become Nation Builders.

My students are top people in their respective fields.

Each student becomes a great world leader.

I am unbiased to all students.

I am aware of my teachings.

I teach them to make more money.

I also make a lot of money.

So be it.

Thank you. Thank you. Thank you.

Done. Done. Done.

<u>Affirmations for Moto GP Racer</u>

I love racing bikes.

I am a world champion racer.

I am next Rossi.

My timings are improving after each race.

I run the race in my mind one day before

that I win the race the next day.

I visualize being a winner.

I love superbikes.

Companies like Honda & Ducati gave me an offer.

I earn millions of dollars every season.

I have won the Road Racing World Championship.

I am promoted to MotoGP Class.

I have never imposed a Long Lap fine.

All records are broken by me.

I am a true MotoGP leader.

My heart beats with my intention.

I use my Power of Intention to win the race.

I won the Qatar Motorcycle Grand Prix.

I won the Argentine Motorcycle Grand Prix.

I won the Motorcycle Grand Prix of Americas.

I won Spanish Motorcycle Grand Prix.

I won French Motorcycle Grand Prix.

I won Italian Motorcycle Grand Prix.

I won the Catalane Motorcycle Grand Prix.

I won German Motorcycle Grand Prix.

I won Czech Republic Motorcycle Grand Prix.

I won Australian Motorcycle Grand Prix.

I won British Motorcycle Grand Prix.

I won Dutch TT.

I won the Riminis Coast Motorcycle Grand Prix.

I won Austrian Motorcycle Grand Prix.

I won the Aragon Motorcycle Grand Prix.

I won the Thailand Motorcycle Grand Prix.

I won Japanese Motorcycle Grand Prix.

I won the Valencian Community Grand Prix.

I won Malaysian Motorcycle Grand Prix.

I am the World Greatest Ever Born Racer.

So be it.

Thank you. Thank you. Thank you.

Done. Done. Done.

<u>Affirmations for Army Officer</u>

I am an Army Officer.

I love my country.

I know my duties.

I respect my countrymen.

My life is for my country.

Country comes first.

I also know my duties towards my family.

I am connected to my family soulfully.

I am the best officer.

I give my best daily.

I will go to heaven after my life.

A soldier's life is a beautiful life.

People love Army men.

I obey the orders of my seniors.

My whole life is dedicated to the nation.

I am born to be a Soldier.

So be it.

Thank you. Thank you. Thank you.

Done. Done. Done.

<u>Affirmations for Air force Pilot</u>

I am a great Fighter Pilot.

I love flying.

I always dreamed of becoming a Pilot.

I am fearless.

Flying is my passion.

I fly like a bird in the air.

Flying is living.

I love my Air Force.

I know my duties very well.

I fly only on directed airfields.

I follow my orders.

I know each and every detail of my aircraft.

Flying is natural to me.

Life as a Pilot is a blessing.

I take all safety precautions before flight.

I was born to be a Pilot.

So be it.

Thank you. Thank you. Thank you.

Done. Done. Done.

<u>Affirmations for Navy Captain</u>

I love sailing.

I always dreamed of becoming a Naval Officer.

I did my best in training.

I am the best in the Navy.

I love the color of the uniform.

White color suits me.

I love sea waters.

I am fond of sea journeys.

Sailing in the ocean is like meeting me.

I am a disciplined Sailor.

I am blessed to be a Naval Officer.

I am a good commander.

My family likes my job.

Life is a great dream.

The East or west Navy is the best.

I was born to be a Naval Officer.

So be it.

Thank you. Thank you. Thank you.

Done. Done. Done.

<u>Affirmations for Professional Trainer</u>

I am a good trainer.

I have identified my training needs successfully.

I am fully prepared for training delivery.

I am ready to change and adapt.

I am always thinking while speaking.

I communicate clearly at all times.

I practice good time management.

I have the confidence to speak in public.

I have the ability to remain focused.

I design effective training programmes.

My training programmes are engaging.

I am able to handle difficult situations.

I am able to handle complex group dynamics.

I have understanding of the subject matter.

I evaluate the outcome of training programmes.

I sell my programmes at good cost.

So be it.

Thank you. Thank you. Thank you.

Done. Done. Done.

<u>Affirmations for Yoga Teacher</u>

I love Yoga.

I am a good Yoga Teacher.

No matter what is the size of the yoga class

I connect to each participant.

I make everyone feel comfortable.

I touch the heart of the participant's every time.

I command the attention of the participants.

I have a natural confidence.

I have a good sense of humor.

I have a light hearted approach.

I am focused.

I am calm.

I am centered.

I am enthusiastic to teach.

I create a peaceful environment in the class.

I bless each participant.

I have my own style.

I surrender to higher energy to pass

through me to the participants.

I am flexible.

I use my intuition to look

for feedback from participants.

Yoga aims to improve the body, mind and spirit.

I pass on the energy from me to participants.

I look at each participant attentively.

I demonstrate knowledge to my participants.

I take care of my participants.

I sell my programs at good cost.

I earn a lot in each session.

So be it.

Thank you. Thank you. Thank you.

Done. Done. Done.

<u>Affirmations for Healer</u>

I love to heal people.

I am a highly sensitive person.

I have an innate quality of being a healer.

People are happy after getting results.

People thank me a lot.

People refer their friends & relatives for healing.

I have the abilities of empathy.

People like to open up with me.

I feel people's emotions.

I am intuitive and can read others easily.

I am a "big picture" thinker.

I am a natural peace maker.

I am aware of the interconnectedness of life.

I believe in synchronicity rather than coincidence.

I am a compassionate and patient listener.

I am a great healer.

So be it.

Thank you. Thank you. Thank you.

Done. Done. Done.

<u>Affirmations for Tarot Reader</u>

I love to be a Tarot Reader.

I am an expert Tarot Card Reader.

I have an open mind before reading.

I trust my instincts while picking a card.

I read the card deep with the heart.

People need my support & reassurances.

I have a good understanding of the tarot cards.

I love what I do and I do it daily.

I have good intuition.

I am gentle, compassionate and fair.

I get a great glimpse of the future.

I speak only after thinking twice to the client.

I have a caring and open heart.

I am true to myself and others.

I have clear intentions of helping people.

I am a great Tarot Reader.

So be it.

Thank you. Thank you. Thank you.

Done. Done. Done.

AFFIRMATIONS FOR BANKERS

I am a good banker.

I do my service with all my heart.

I come to the office on time.

I finish my work daily.

My desk is always clean.

I am well dressed.

I talk to my customers politely.

I am a gentleman.

I had a happy time with my family.

I speak positively about my organization.

I go home on time daily.

I keep myself healthy and fit.

I avail all my benefits and leisure.

Work is worship for me.

I am in tune with the vision, mission

and values of the organization.

My life rotates around banking.

I eat, think and dream about my bank.

I delegate my duties more than 100%.

I go by the system and procedure.

I am ethical and loyal to the bank.

All loans, deposits & other works are profitable to me.

I invest my money in bank's shares.

I grew with the bank.

Regular transfers open my personality.

I am an honest banker.

I am my bank.

So be it

Thank you Thank you Thank you

Done Done Done.

AFFIRMATIONS FOR SINGERS

I am a great singer.

My voice is magnificent.

My vocal cords vibrate properly.

I take care of my voice.

My voice has depth.

I do exercise daily.

My Pituitary Gland sends a powerful voice.

My voice is wonderful.

People love my voice.

I have a command in my voice.

My voice reaches every corner of the stadium.

People hear me patiently.

Proper and clear words come out of my mouth.

I am an expert in voice articulation.

I know which voice comes from where.

My voice is clear.

Microphone loves my voice.

Music composers want me to sing for them.

My songs are at No.1 position in chartbusters.

The whole world sings and loves my songs.

All radio channels of the Radio Garden app

prefer to play my song.

People sing my songs in groups and parties.

Each farewell has at least one of my songs.

People remember me as a legend.

God sings through me.

My voice attracts my listeners.

My songs sell well.

My distribution company loves my work.

I am a highly paid singer.

So be it

Thank you Thank you Thank you

Done Done Done.

AFFIRMATIONS FOR STUDENTS

I am an IITian.

I have qualified for the IIT in my first attempt.

I have got my favorite stream and subjects.

My coaching teachers are proud of me.

My parents are proud of me.

I am an inspiration to other aspirants.

It's my dream to get into IIT.

I got the IIT of my choice.

My marks were extraordinary.

Questions always come in my dreams.

All questions were already practiced by me.

I know each and every answer.

I completed my exam on time.

I was sure that I would qualify for the JEE Exam.

IIT is now my reality.

I have worked for it.

I will make use of studying in IIT.

I will start my business.

I will make my country proud.

I will be innovative in approach.

So be it

Thank you Thank you Thank you

Done Done Done.

AFFIRMATIONS FOR TELECALLERS

I love telecalling.

I daily do at least ten calls.

In a month I do more than 300 calls.

I get my leads from my friends.

All my leads are converted.

Parents talk to us with patience.

Parents listen to us patiently.

All parents want to see growth in their kids.

Parents respond to us well.

They are happy to pay for the snack box.

Parents are convinced by us.

Parents decided to join the programme.

Parents come with their payment options.

Parents want their children to excel.

Parents are convinced within the seminar.

Parents come with a mindset to invest.

Parents like the concept and are ready.

Parents are excited. Children are excited.

God bless parents and their children.

So be it

Thank you Thank you Thank you

Done Done Done.

AFFIRMATION FOR DOCTORS

I am a Doctor.

I have qualified for a medical exam.

I got my favorite institute.

I got my chosen subject.

I am good at learning skills.

My exam paper appeared in my dreams.

All questions were already known to me.

I scored great marks in the final exam.

I qualified for the medical exam on merit.

I am proud of myself.

My teachers are proud of me.

My parents are proud of me.

I love being a Doctor.

I will serve my patients.

I am serving my countrymen.

I get National and International awards.

My photographs are published in the newspaper.

I lead a happy life.

So be it.

Thank you Thank you Thank you.

Done Done Done.

<u>AFFIRMATION FOR IAS OFFICER</u>

I am an IAS officer.

I have qualified for my exam.

My training is at IAS Academy Mussoorie.

I have scored good marks.

I qualified for the prelims exam.

I qualified for the mains exam.

I got perfect coaching for the UPSC exam.

I knew almost all the answers in the exam.

My teachers guided me perfectly,

My life goal is serving INDIA.

I love to be an IAS officer.

My childhood dream is now the reality of my life.

My photo and interview is published in newspapers.

My coaching institute has awarded me.

I am an inspiration to others.

My roll number appeared in the final list.

My dream has come true.

I have done it.

So be it.

Thank you Thank you Thank you.

Done. Done . Done.

AFFIRMATION FOR BEAUTY

I am Beautiful

I love a beautiful soul.

I have a beautiful heart.

I have a beautiful mind.

My thinking is beautiful

My personality is beautiful.

My physique is attractive.

My feelings are beautiful.

My expressions are beautiful.

My desires are beautiful.

Beauty lies in each cell of my body.

Beauty vibrates from my whole being.

Being beautiful is one of my priorities.

My beauty lies deep in my skin.

Whole universe is beautiful.

Energy is beautiful and I am energy.

I always work on my beauty.

I am beautiful.

So be it.

Thank you. Thank you. Thank you.

Done. Done. Done.

AFFIRMATION FOR GETTING MARRIED

I am married.

I am a great partner.

My partner is ideal.

We support each other.

We share a lot about ourselves.

We give space to each other.

We promote each other.

I have got a best friend in my partner.

My all desires are fulfilled now.

My partner motivates me.

My life has become beautiful.

My partner fulfills me.

Life has become magical after I met my partner.

Marriage is bliss to me.

I am no longer a loner.

We spend quality time with each other.

There is faith and trust among us.

We are one.

So be it.

Thank you Thank you Thank you

Done. Done. Done.

AFFIRMATION FOR BEAUTIFUL EYES

I have beautiful eyes.

My eyes are the window of my soul.

I keep my eyes healthy.

I do Eyes Yoga regularly.

My eyesight is perfect.

My eyelashes have become dark.

My eyes attract people.

My eyes show them that I am honest.

People love the confidence in my shiny eyes.

My eyes are magnetic.

My eyes rested in sleep.

My eyes are fearless.

People are hypnotized by my eyes.

I always have a deep sleep.

My eyes show love and respect to others.

My eyes are convincing.

My eyes are attractive.

I love my eyes.

So be it.

Thank you. Thank you. Thank you.

Done. Done. Done.

AFFIRMATION FOR CHILD

I love my child.

My child is the best.

I will do everything for the child.

My child is unique.

My child has great potential.

My child will make history.

I know about the intelligence in my child.

I will upgrade my child's potential.

My child always remains high energy.

My child has a creative mind.

My child learns very fast.

My child is honest with me.

My child is well mannered.

Everything is possible for my child.

My child receives the best training.

We know our child's inclination.

My child is all rounder.

My child works on special talents.

My child is a great soul.

My child has good height.

My child is healthy.

My child is sporty.

My child is good at academics.

My child is good at extracurricular activities.

My child is God's blessing.

So be it

Thank you Thank you Thank you

Done Done Done.

9 798504 287980